Welcome to My Home!

Contents

Written by Catherine Baker

Collins

Welcome to our homes!

Come and see our homes!

Jodie, China

I'm Jodie!

It has big windows, so I can see the crowded street!

Helping at home

I like helping to wash up!

Out and about

There is a forest near home! We ride bikes on the trails.

We hear music in the streets.

I like samba music!

We get snacks from street stalls.

crisp little fish balls

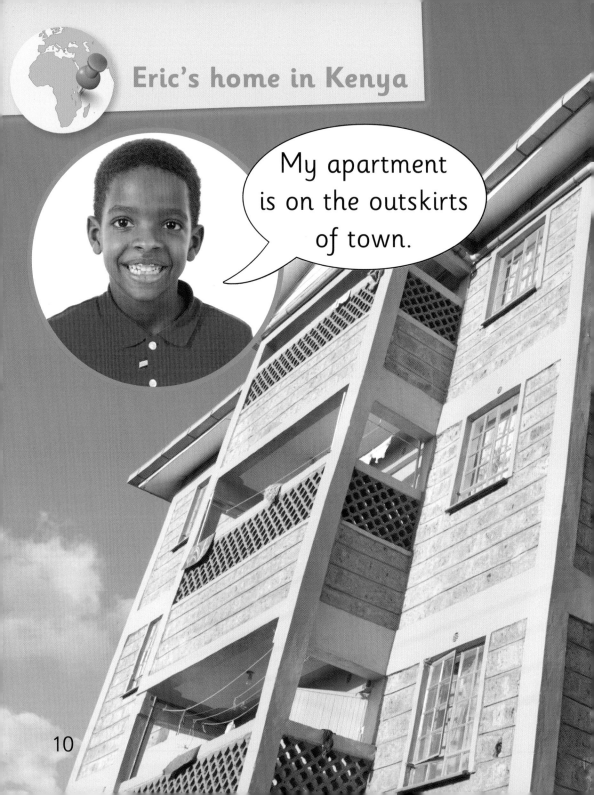

My apartment is on the outskirts of town.

The big shopping mall is near us!

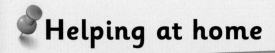

Helping at home

I help clear up after lunch.

I love all sports – but football is the best!

A day out

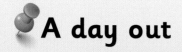

For a treat, we go to the animal park.

14

We get skewers of meat
as a snack.

My home is in this apartment.

16

There are crowds of other children to play with!

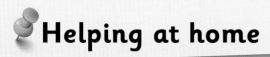

Helping at home

I help to keep my bedroom clean and smart.

18

Food

I love clear chicken soup with greens.

We like floating in a pedal boat!

A day out

We take the tram up to the Peak.

The Peak is the top of a steep hill

21

Compare the homes

homes

food

helping

fun

23

After reading

Letters and Sounds: Phase 5

Word count: 223

Focus phonemes: /igh/ i, i-e /ai/ ay, a-e /oa/ o, ow, o-e /oo/ u, ew, ou /ee/ ie, ea /ow/ ou /ar/ a /or/ al /air/ ere /u/ o-e /o/ a

Common exception words: of, to, the, are, my, we, so, little, our

Curriculum links: Geography

National Curriculum learning objectives: Reading/word reading: read accurately by blending sounds in unfamiliar words containing GPCs that have been taught; read words containing taught GPCs and -s, ... -ing, -ed, ... endings; Reading/comprehension: link what they read or hear read to their own experiences

Developing fluency

- Take turns to read a page of text. Use a narrator's more formal tone for the chapter titles, subheadings and labels; use a more enthusiastic, expressive voice for each child in the book.
- Ask your child to locate a section using the contents list and headings, then read that section aloud. For example, say: Can you find and read the section about Ana?; Can you find and read the section about Eric?

Phonic practice

- Challenge your child to find words in the book with -s, -ing and -ed endings and to read them aloud:
  o -s (e.g. page 4 **flats**, page 5 **windows**, page 7 **trails**, page 8 **streets**, page 10 **outskirts**)
  o -ing (pages 6, 12, 18, 23 **helping**, page 11 **shopping**, page 20 **floating**)
  o -ed: (page 5 **crowded**)
- Ask your child to find words that contain the /oa/ phoneme (**home, go, windows**) and the /oo/ phoneme (**music, new, soup**) and discuss their different spellings.

Extending vocabulary

- Look at page 5 and point to the word **crowded**. Ask: Can you think of a word with an opposite meaning? (e.g. *deserted, empty, bare*)
- Repeat for the following:
  o page 7 **trails** (e.g. *paths, walkways, roads*)
  o page 10 **outskirts** (e.g. *edges, suburbs, outside*)